# Maths all around you

# FRACTIONS

**Rob Colson**

WAYLAND

First published in Great Britain
in 2025 by Wayland
Copyright © Hodder and Stoughton Limited, 2025
All rights reserved

Series editor: Amy Pimperton
Designed and edited by Tall Tree Ltd
Consultant: Jim Newall
Artist: Joseph Wilkins/Beehive Art Agency

HB ISBN: 978 1 5263 2049 0
PB ISBN: 978 1 5263 2050 6

Wayland
An imprint of Hachette Children's Group
Part of Hodder and Stoughton
Carmelite House
50 Victoria Embankment
London EC4Y 0DZ

An Hachette UK Company
www.hachette.co.uk
www.hachettechildrens.co.uk

Printed and bound in China

Picture Credits
FC-front cover, BC-back cover, t-top, b-bottom, l-left, r-right, c-centre
1–48 Sandra_M/Shutterstock.com, 4bl Maksim Shmeljov/Shutterstock.com, 5tr Daniliuc Victor/Shutterstock.com, 5br PTZ Pictures/Shutterstock.com, 5bl creator12/Shutterstock.com, 6tl Evannovostro/Shutterstock.com, 6bl Peter Sobolev/ Shutterstock.com, 7c VectorMine/Shutterstock.com, 9tr Kozak Sergii/Shutterstock.com, 9cr Ljupco Smokovski/Shutterstock.com, 9b Dmytro Zinkevych/Shutterstock.com, 10–11 Voyagerix/Shutterstock. com, 11br David Antonio Lopez Moya/Shutterstock.com, 12bl Dervish45/Shutterstock.com, 12b JeepFoto/Shutterstock.com, 14tl CK Foto/Shutterstock.com, 14b Sion Hannuna/Shutterstock.com, 15tr Jason Finn/Shutterstock.com, 15cr podtin/Shutterstock.com, 15bl Christine Bird/Shutterstock.com, 16c Pit Stock/Shutterstock.com, 17l Debbie Oetgen/Shutterstock.com, 17c wiangya/Shutterstock.com, 18c Gregory J Smith/Shutterstock.com, 18b Jodie Johnson/Shutterstock.com, 18br Pascale Gueret/ Shutterstock.com, 19tl Ryan R Fox/Shutterstock.com, 19c Irina Mos/Shutterstock.com, 20c Sur/ Shutterstock.com, 20–21b Luke Schmidt/Shutterstock.com, 21t INTREEGUE Photography/Shutterstock.com, 22t IZZ HAZEL/Shutterstock.com, 22b LO Kin-hei/Shutterstock.com, 23tr Frederico Rostagno/Shutterstock. com, 23tl Shutterstock.com/Love Lego, 23cr Alvov/Shutterstock.com, 23b Kuleshov Oleg/Shutterstock. com, 24tl Isaac Crabtree/Shutterstock.com, 24b mRGB/Shutterstock.com, 25c Nightman1965/ Shutterstock.com, 25bl Songquan Deng/Shutterstock.com, 25br Mr. Amarin Jitnathum/Shutterstock. com, 26t Maksim Safaniuk/Shutterstock.com, 26b Gill Copeland/Shutterstock.com, 27t sakoat contributor/Shutterstock.com, 27b Stockr/Shutterstock.com, 28c EMFA16/Shutterstock.com, 29t Rudmer Zwerver/Shutterstock.com, 29br Foto-Ruhrgebiet/Shutterstock.com, 30t Rudy Balasko/ Shutterstock.com, 30bl Gladysh Alexsandr/Shutterstock.com, 30br GREENWALDOS/Shutterstock. com, 31t aSuruwataRi/Shutterstock.com, 30–31c jamesteohart/Shutterstock.com, 32l SvedOliver/ Shutterstock.com, 32r Markus Mainka/Shutterstock.com, 32b Sukpaiboonwat/Shutterstock.com, 33c Vera Larina/Shutterstock.com, 34c NChutchikov/Shutterstock.com, 35t Waldis Putnis/Shutterstock. com, 35bl Douglas Cliff/Shutterstock.com, 36c tele52/Shutterstock.com

# CONTENTS

# What is a fraction?

**A fraction is a part of a whole. In maths, fractions are parts of whole numbers that have been split up into equal pieces.**

A fraction is written with two numbers.

The top number, called the **numerator**, is the number of pieces we have.

The bottom number, called the **denominator**, is the number of pieces in the whole.

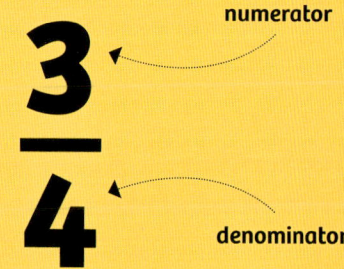

$$\frac{3}{4}$$

numerator

denominator

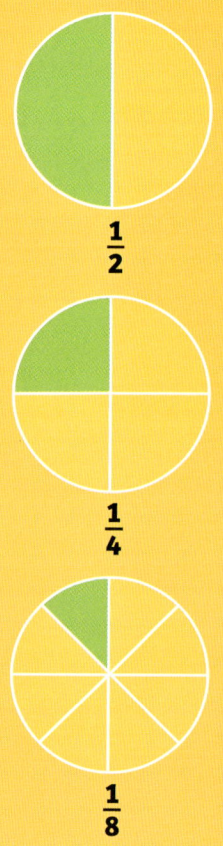

$\frac{1}{2}$

$\frac{1}{4}$

$\frac{1}{8}$

This pizza has been split into eight pieces, or eighths. If two slices are eaten, then six eighths are left. This can be written as the fraction $\frac{6}{8}$.

Fractions are said to be **equivalent** if they represent the same amount as one another.

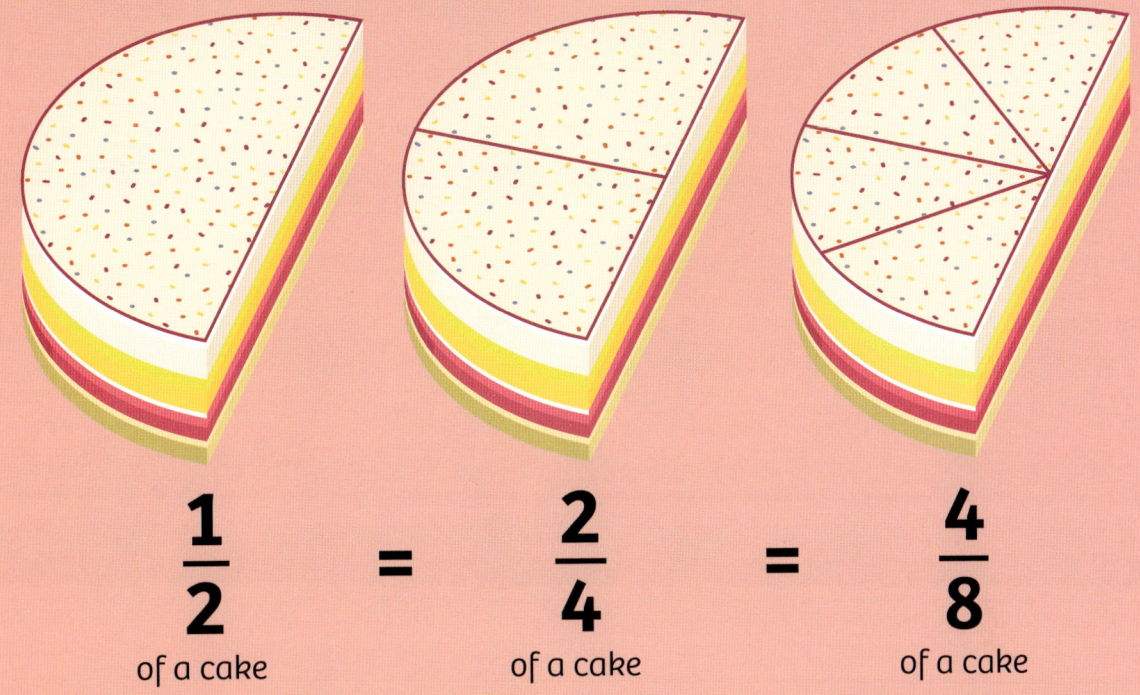

$$\frac{1}{2} = \frac{2}{4} = \frac{4}{8}$$

of a cake    of a cake    of a cake

# Try this!

Which of the groups of slices below add up to half a pizza?

## Try this!

Throughout the book, there are puzzles for you to solve. Keep a pencil and notebook handy to write your answers in.

a)

b)

c)

Answers on page 47

# Mixed numbers and improper fractions

**Mixed numbers** are numbers that combine a whole number with a fraction. Mixed numbers can also be written as **improper fractions**. These are fractions whose numerator is larger than the denominator.

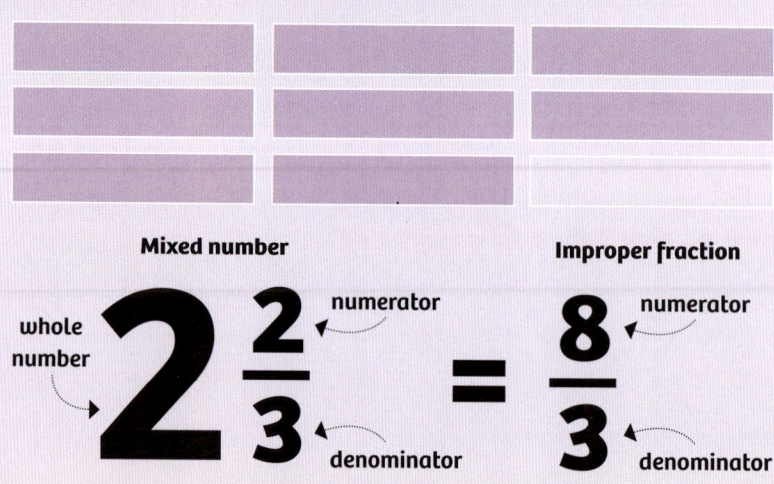

Mixed number

whole number

$2\frac{2}{3}$

numerator

denominator

Improper fraction

$= \frac{8}{3}$

numerator

denominator

$2\frac{1}{2}$ biscuits

## Mixed numbers around us

In everyday life, we usually use mixed numbers more than improper fractions. For example, if you are sharing five biscuits between two people, you can have $2\frac{1}{2}$ biscuits each. There is no need to break all the biscuits in half to make $\frac{5}{2}$ biscuits each!

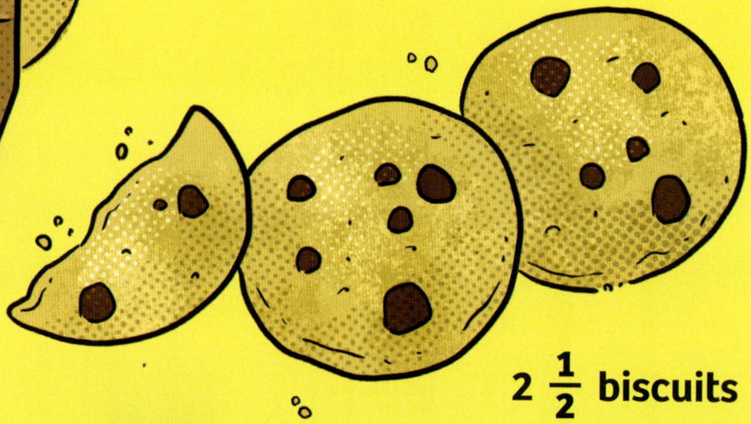

$2\frac{1}{2}$ biscuits

A proper fraction is less than 1.

$$\frac{1}{2}$$

An improper fraction is greater than 1.

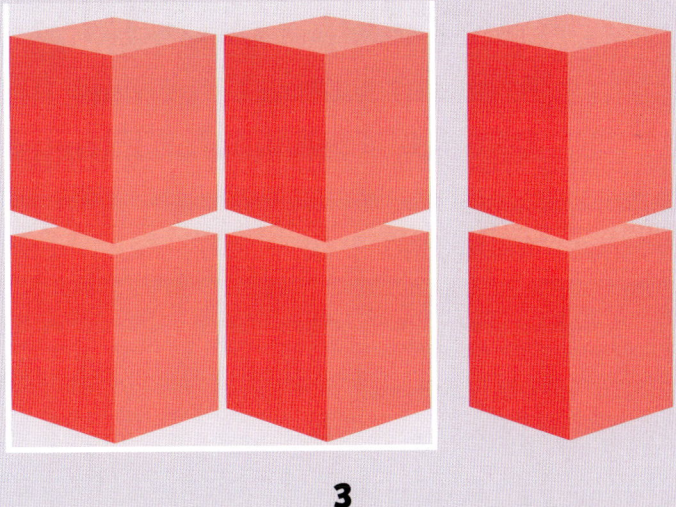

$$\frac{3}{2}$$

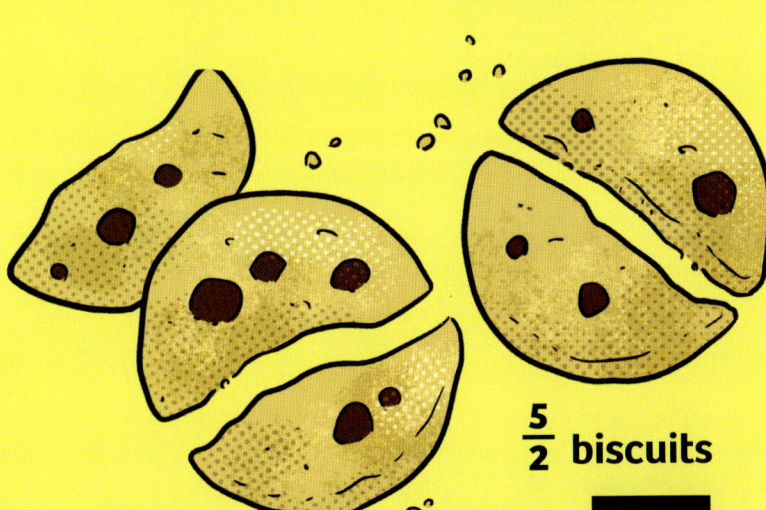

$\frac{5}{2}$ biscuits

$\frac{5}{2}$ biscuits

## What examples of mixed numbers can you see around you?

### Try this!

1. Convert these improper fractions into mixed numbers.

a) $\frac{7}{5}$　　b) $\frac{103}{9}$　　c) $\frac{26}{7}$

2. Convert these mixed numbers into improper fractions.

a) $4\frac{3}{7}$　　b) $22\frac{1}{2}$

c) $3\frac{8}{9}$

Answers on page 47

# Adding and subtracting fractions

To add or subtract fractions, first you need to find their common denominator, if they don't have one already.

For example, to add $\frac{1}{3}$ to $\frac{1}{5}$, give both fractions a denominator of 15, then add:

$\frac{1}{3}$ + $\frac{1}{5}$ =

$\frac{5}{15}$ + $\frac{3}{15}$ =

$\frac{8}{15}$

To subtract one fraction from another, you follow the same rules as for addition:

$$\frac{1}{3} - \frac{1}{5} = \frac{5}{15} - \frac{3}{15} = \frac{2}{15}$$

# Domino fractions

Dominoes have two numbers on them with a line in between. If you turn a domino vertically, you create a fun fraction! These three dominoes show equivalent fractions.

## Can you find more equivalent fractions in a set of dominoes? What is the smallest fraction you can make?

# Tricks for adding fractions

Try this simple trick for adding and subtracting **two** fractions with different denominators.

$$\frac{1}{2} + \frac{1}{3} = ?$$

**1.** First, multiply the denominators by one another to find the common denominator:

**2.** Multiply the left numerator by the right denominator and write this in the numerator of the answer.

**3.** Now, multiply the right numerator by the left denominator and add this number to the numerator in the answer.

$$\frac{1}{2} + \frac{1}{3} = \frac{\phantom{3}}{6}$$

$$\frac{1}{2} + \frac{1}{3} = \frac{3}{6}$$

$$\frac{1}{2} + \frac{1}{3} = \frac{3+2}{6}$$

## ... and the answer is

$$\frac{1}{2} + \frac{1}{3} = \frac{3+2}{6} = \frac{5}{6}$$

This method also works for subtraction:

$$\frac{1}{2} - \frac{1}{3} = \frac{3-2}{6} = \frac{1}{6}$$

## Try this!

*Complete the following calculations.*

a) $\frac{1}{3} + \frac{1}{4} = ?$

b) $\frac{3}{4} - \frac{1}{5} = ?$

Answers on page 47

# Multiplying and dividing fractions

Knowing how to multiply with fractions helps when you need to divide up collections of things.

Multiplying a fraction by a whole number is equivalent to adding the fraction to itself that number of times.

$$\frac{1}{4} \times 3 = \frac{1}{4} + \frac{1}{4} + \frac{1}{4} = \frac{3}{4}$$

The rule for multiplying any fraction by a whole number is that you multiply the **numerator** of the fraction by the whole number.

$$\frac{2}{3} \times 4 = \frac{2 \times 4}{3} = \frac{8}{3} = 2\frac{2}{3}$$

To divide a fraction by a whole number, multiply the **denominator** of the fraction by the whole number.

$$\frac{2}{3} \div 4 = \frac{2}{3 \times 4} = \frac{2}{12} = \frac{1}{6}$$

# Multiplying fractions by fractions

To multiply a fraction by another fraction, you multiply the denominators and multiply the numerators.

$$\frac{4}{5} \times \frac{2}{3} = \frac{4 \times 2}{5 \times 3} = \frac{8}{15}$$

**Fractions are useful when you want to share things fairly. When have you used fractions to share with your friends?**

## Try this!

**1.** Melody's farm is divided into 5 fields of equal size. She wants to graze her 9 horses and grow vegetables. If each horse needs $\frac{1}{3}$ of a field on which to graze, **how many fields can Melody use to grow vegetables?**

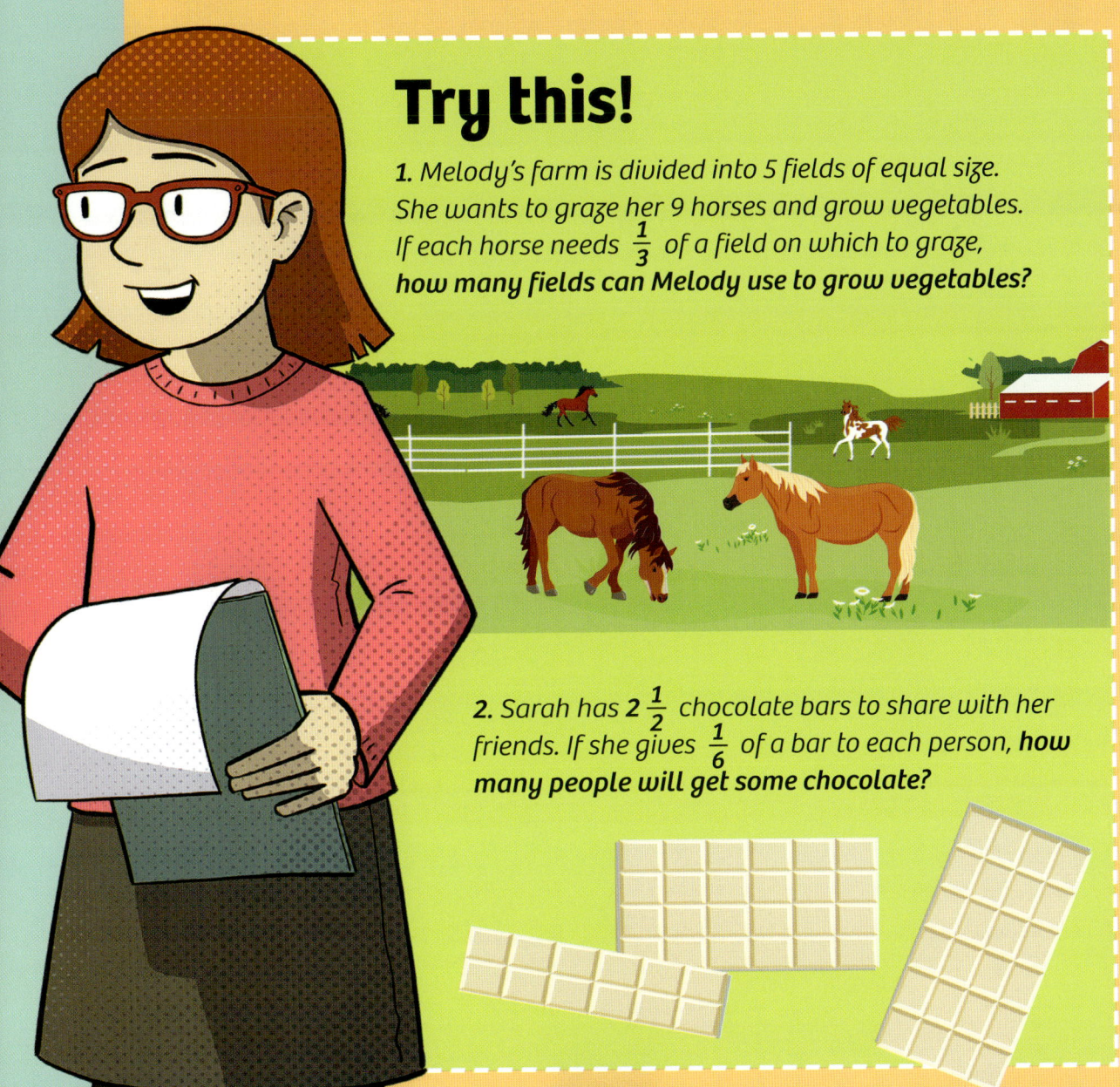

**2.** Sarah has $2\frac{1}{2}$ chocolate bars to share with her friends. If she gives $\frac{1}{6}$ of a bar to each person, **how many people will get some chocolate?**

Answers on page 47

# Fractions on the number line

We often think of fractions as parts of a whole shape. For instance, this circle is split into fractions of seven equal parts. $\frac{1}{7}$ of the circle is coloured red.

## Number lines

It can also be useful in maths to think of fractions as parts of a number line that extends from 0 on the left to 1 on the right.

0    $\frac{1}{7}$    $\frac{2}{7}$    $\frac{3}{7}$    $\frac{4}{7}$    $\frac{5}{7}$    $\frac{6}{7}$    1

*Here, the number line is divided into seven equal sections. The fraction $\frac{1}{7}$ is represented by the first section, while all seven sections represent $\frac{7}{7}$, or 1.*

*Writing out number lines for different denominators shows us which fractions are bigger than others. Here are the fractions with denominators 2 to 8 on their number lines.*

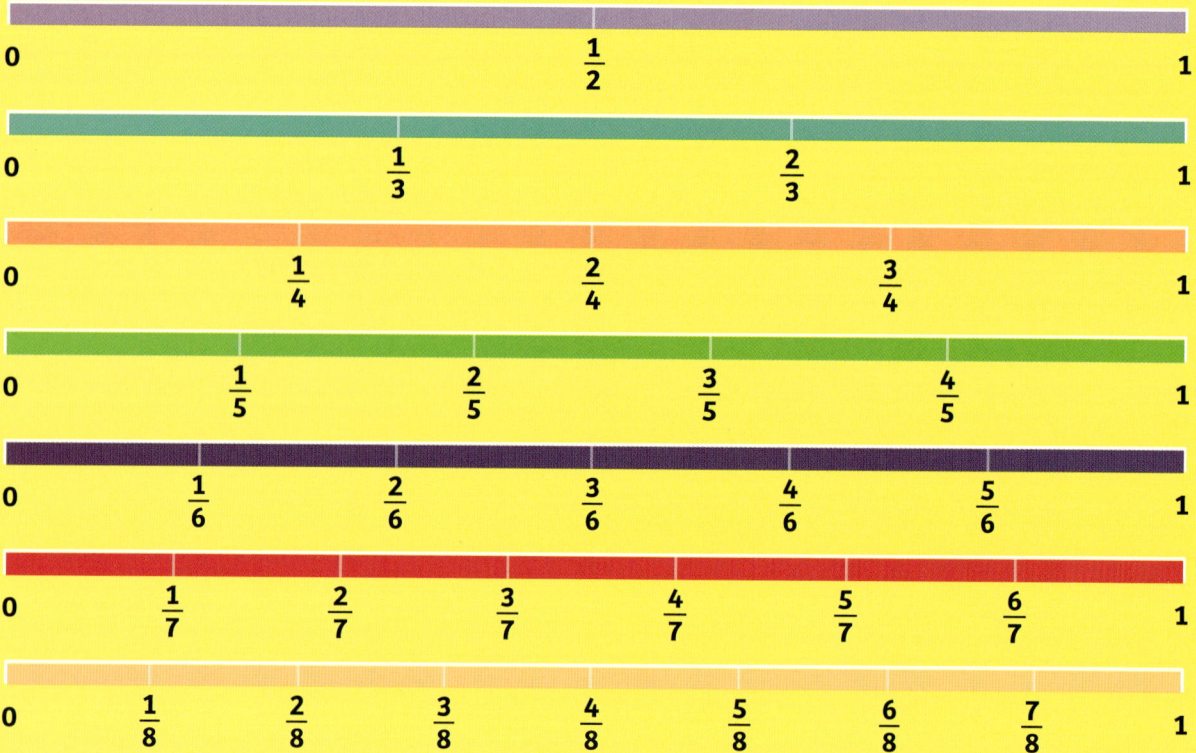

*By looking at the number line, you can easily see that $\frac{2}{3}$ is larger than $\frac{3}{5}$, while $\frac{2}{8}$ is an equivalent fraction to $\frac{1}{4}$.*

12

# Number lines around you

A ruler is a straight number line, with centimetres and millimetres (tenths of centimetres) marked on it. Number lines can also be curved.

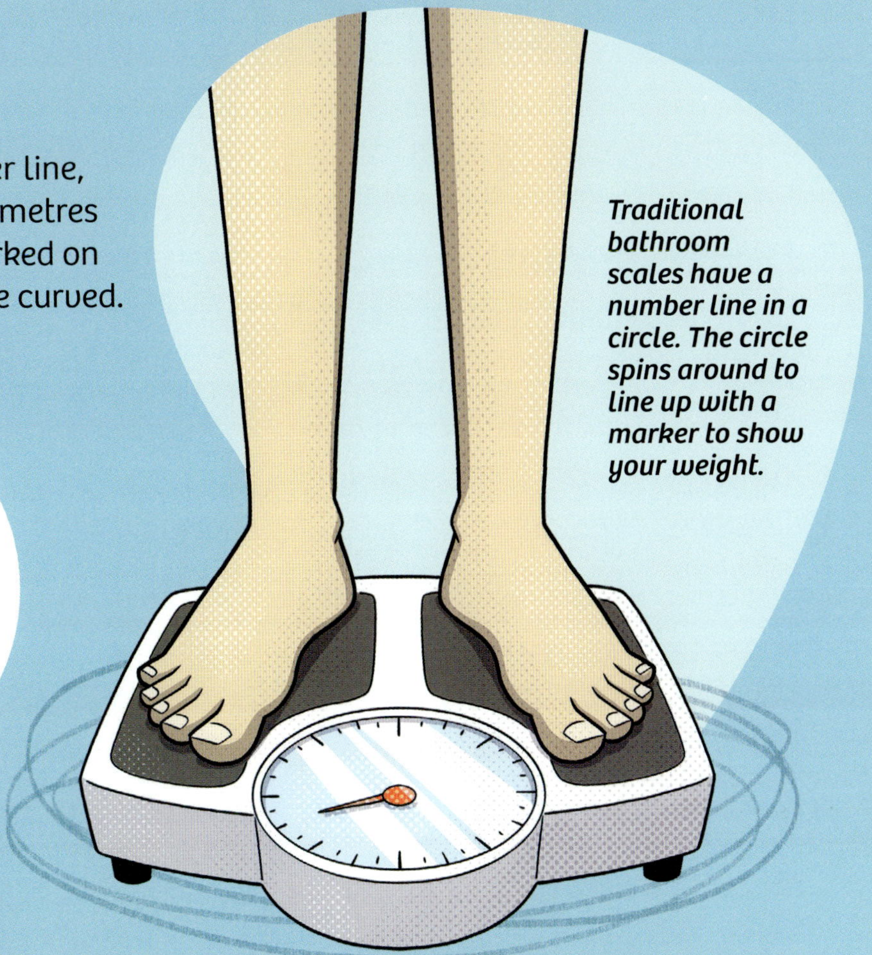

*Traditional bathroom scales have a number line in a circle. The circle spins around to line up with a marker to show your weight.*

*A car's fuel gauge is a curved number line showing fractions of a full tank of fuel. The gauge above shows fifths.*

# Try this!

*Many rulers have two scales on them – centimetres along one side and inches along the other. Find a ruler with both scales.* **What fraction is the inch number line divided into? Is this different from the centimetre number line?** *Use a ruler with both scales to answer the following.*

**a) To the nearest tenth, how many centimetres are there in one inch?**

**b) Which is the longer length: $\frac{1}{4}$ inch or $\frac{1}{2}$ centimetre?**

Answers on page 47

# Decimal fractions

**Decimal fractions are fractions with a denominator that is a power of 10.**

## Decimal point

Decimal fractions can be written using a decimal point.

zero units

six tenths

$$\frac{67}{100} = 0.67$$

decimal point

seven hundredths

To convert a fraction into a decimal fraction, you need to find the equivalent fraction with a denominator that is a power of 10.

$$\frac{1}{2} = \frac{5}{10} = 0.5 \qquad \frac{2}{5} = \frac{4}{10} = 0.4 \qquad \frac{1}{8} = \frac{125}{1000} = 0.125$$

## Decimal fractions around us

Money is usually divided up into decimal fractions. For instance, £1 is divided into 100 pence, while $1 is divided into 100 cents. When writing money fractions, the number of hundredths is always written down, even if it is zero. For instance, 10 pence equals £0.10.

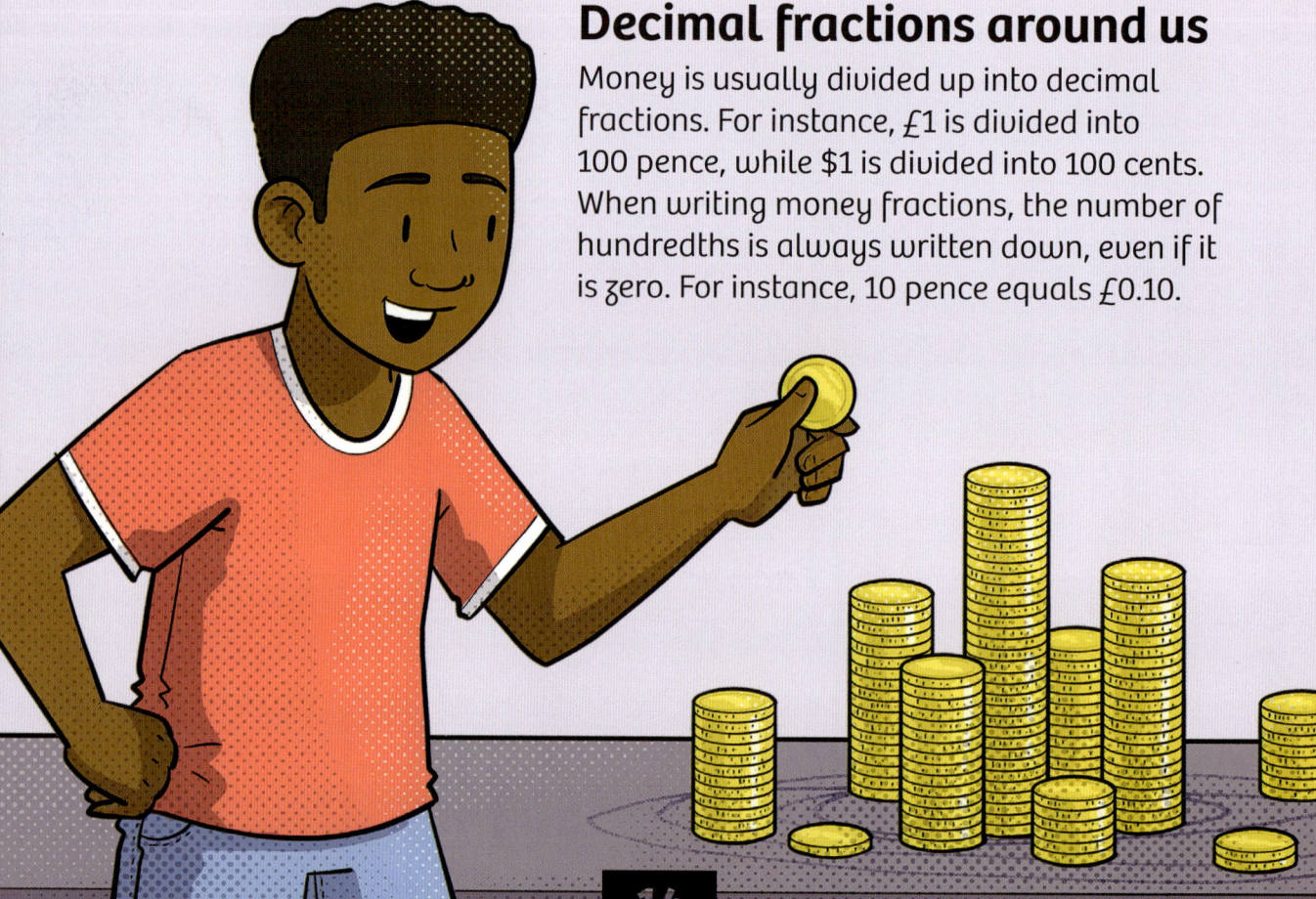

**'Power of 10'** means 10 multiplied by itself a number of times.

$$10 \times 1 = 10$$
$$\frac{1}{10} = 1 \text{ tenth} = 0.1$$

$$10 \times 10 = 100$$
$$\frac{1}{100} = 1 \text{ hundredth} = 0.01$$

$$10 \times 10 \times 10 = 1000$$
$$\frac{1}{1000} = 1 \text{ thousandth} = 0.001$$

Sometimes you cannot turn a fraction into an exact decimal.

$\frac{1}{3}$ (one third) is an example.

When you turn $\frac{1}{3}$ into a decimal, you get 0.333…, where '…' means 'recurring', or going on for ever.

Other recurring decimals include:

$\frac{1}{9}$ = 0.111… (1 recurring)

$\frac{1}{15}$ = 0.0666… (6 recurring).

**£1 coin**

= 10 x £0.10 coins

= 100 x £0.01 coins

# Try this!

*Decimal fractions can be added together following the same rules of addition as the addition of whole numbers. This makes it easier to add up the cost of items.*

*You are at a shop and you have £5 to spend on groceries. Your shopping list includes the items listed to the right.*

| Milk | £0.90 |
| Eggs | £1.50 |
| Bread | £1.60 |

*If an ice lolly costs £0.80, do you have enough money to treat yourself to any? How many ice lollies can you afford to buy?*

Answers on page 47

# Tiny fractions

Sometimes, you need to divide something many times. Tiny decimal fractions are used to measure very small things.

| Fraction | Decimal |
| --- | --- |
| Hundredth | 0.01 |
| Thousandth | 0.001 |
| Millionth | 0.000001 |
| Billionth | 0.000000001 |
| Trillionth | 0.000000000001 |

In the metric measurement scale, there are **100 centimetres** in **1 metre**. There are **1,000 millimetres** in **1 metre**.

## Tiny fractions around you

The average width of a human hair is about 50 millionths of a metre.

Single-cell bacteria are about 1 millionth of a metre across — too small to see with the naked eye.

The smallest object that it is possible to see under a microscope is an atom measuring 0.1 billionths of a metre across.

# Try this!

Take a piece of A4 paper and fold it in half. Now fold it in half again. Keep on folding the paper in half until you can't do it any more. **How many times can you fold the paper?**

You will find that you cannot fold the paper more than seven times. Each time you fold the paper, you halve its surface area, but you double its thickness. The paper starts off about 0.1 mm thick. After one fold, it is 0.2 mm thick. By the sixth fold, it is 6.4 mm thick and feels very solid. If you could keep on folding, 42 folds would make the paper thick enough to reach the Moon, nearly 400,000 km away!

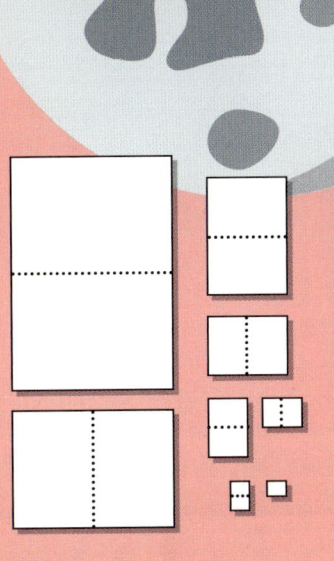

To make accurate experiments, physicists build machines that are capable of measuring distances to the nearest **20 trillionths** of a metre!

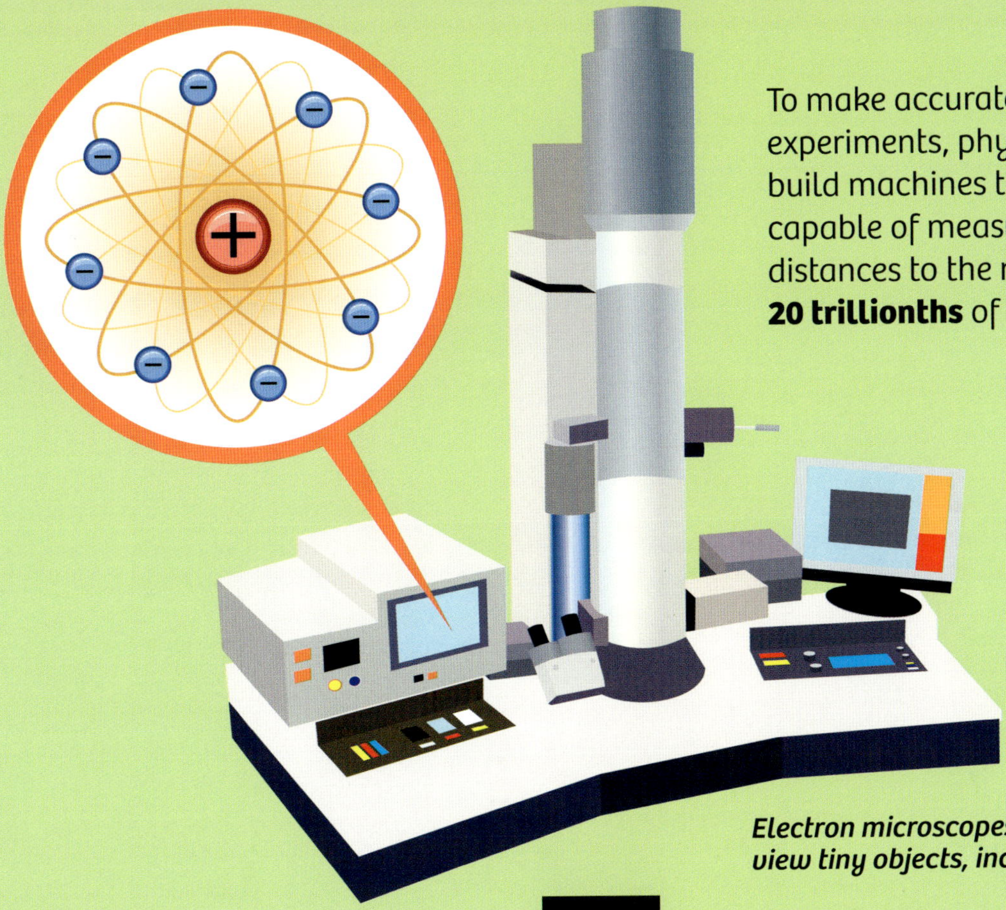

*Electron microscopes are used to view tiny objects, including atoms.*

# Fractions of time

Time is measured in units that are divided into fractions.

**1 hour is**
$$\frac{1}{24}$$
**of a day**

**1 minute is**
$$\frac{1}{60}$$
**of an hour**

**1 second is**
$$\frac{1}{60}$$
**of a minute**

1 day = 24 hours = 1,440 minutes = 86,400 seconds

## Time on a clockface

This clockface has three hands on it.

The second hand completes one full rotation every minute.

The minute hand completes one full rotation every hour. It moves at $\frac{1}{60}$ the speed of the second hand.

The hour hand completes one full rotation every 12 hours. It moves at $\frac{1}{12}$ the speed of the minute hand.

There are 24 hours in a day, so the hour hand fully rotates twice every day.

# Fractions on a clockface

Dividing an hour into 60 minutes is useful because 60 can be exactly divided by 12 different numbers.

**1, 2, 3, 4, 5, 6, 10, 12, 15, 20, 30, 60**

These numbers can be matched up in pairs to give us the number of minutes in half an hour, a third of an hour, a quarter of an hour, and so on.

*1 x 60 = 60*
*1 hour = 60 minutes*

*2 x 30 = 60*
$\frac{1}{2}$ *hour = 30 minutes*

*3 x 20 = 60*
$\frac{1}{3}$ *hour = 20 minutes*

*4 x 15 = 60*
$\frac{1}{4}$ *hour = 15 minutes*

*5 x 12 = 60*
$\frac{1}{5}$ *hour = 12 minutes*

*6 x 10 = 60*
$\frac{1}{6}$ *hour = 10 minutes*

## Try this!

*At rest, your heart beats on average 60–80 times per minute. That's a little over once per second. Check your heart rate by measuring your pulse.*

*Place the index finger of one hand on your opposite wrist just below the thumb. Once you have found your pulse, count the number of beats in 15 seconds. Multiply this number by 4 to give the number of beats per minute.*

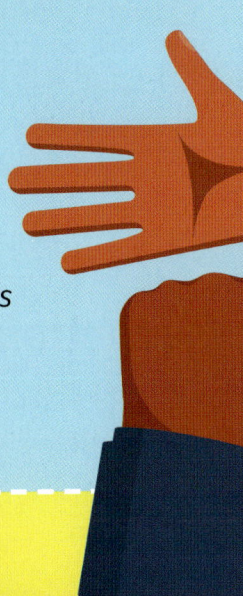

# Fractions of a second

A stopwatch measures fractions of a second using decimal fractions.

In sprint races, such as the 100 metres, times are given to the nearest $\frac{1}{100}$, or 0.01 of a second.

In 2009, Jamaican athlete Usain Bolt set a men's 100 m world record time of **9.58 seconds**.

In 1988, American athlete Florence Griffith-Joyner set a women's 100 m world record time of **10.49 seconds**.

## Tiny fractions

A millisecond is equal to $\frac{1}{1000}$ of a second, or 0.001 seconds. A nanosecond equals one billionth of a second. That's $\frac{1}{1,000,000,000}$ of a second, or 0.000000001 seconds.

# Fractions of seconds around you

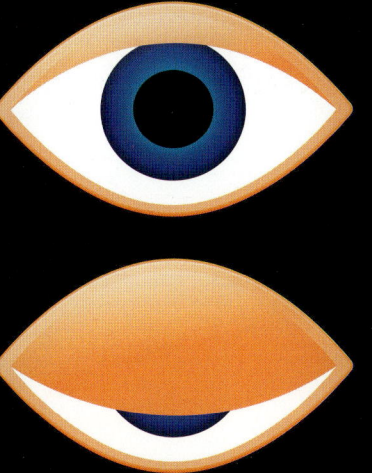

The blink of an eye lasts about 0.1 seconds, or 100 milliseconds.

Most clocks around us, in watches, phones and computers, keep time by dividing a second into tiny fractions and counting these. A quartz crystal inside a clock vibrates when electricity passes through it. The crystal vibrates exactly 32,768 times per second, meaning that a quartz clock is accurate to the nearest $\frac{1}{32,768}$, or 0.00003, of a second!

Computers operate so quickly that their speeds are measured in nanoseconds. The fastest chips inside modern computers can access information in the computer's memory in less than 10 nanoseconds.

**Microchip**

# Try this!

*When you see something happen, it takes a fraction of a second for you to react to it. Compare your reaction times with those of your friends with this simple experiment.*

*Hold a 30 cm ruler out in front of you. Ask a friend to put their thumb and index finger either side of the bottom of the ruler. Tell your friend to catch the ruler as soon as you drop it. Record the measurement on the ruler where your friend catches it. Do this three times and take the average, then swap around. The person with the fastest reaction time is the one with the smallest measurement on the ruler.* **How do your reaction times compare?**

# Counting the days

## Longer periods of time are divided up according to the movements of Earth.

A day is the length of time it takes for Earth to rotate once on its axis.

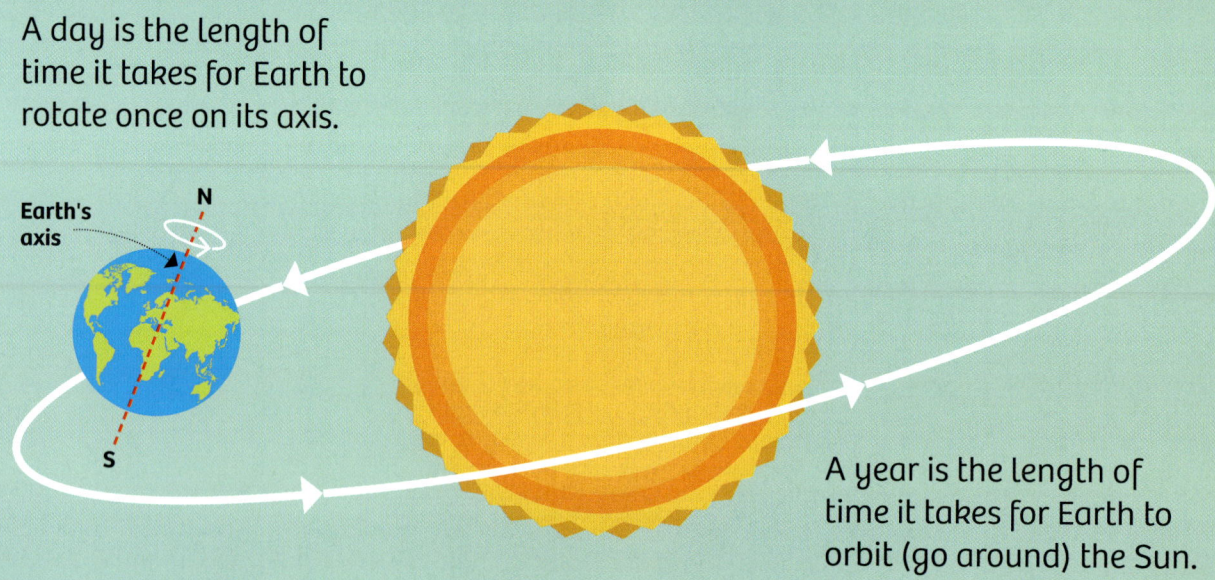

Earth's axis

N

S

A year is the length of time it takes for Earth to orbit (go around) the Sun.

## Leap years

Most years are 365 days long. However, the true length of a year is about **365 $\frac{1}{4}$** days. Every fourth year is a leap year with 366 days.

The exact length of a true year in decimals is 365.2422 days, just under **365 $\frac{1}{4}$** . For this reason, leap years are missed off if the year is divisible by 100, but not if the year is also divisible by 400.

### FEBRUARY

| SUN | MON | TUE | WED | THU | FRI | SAT |
|-----|-----|-----|-----|-----|-----|-----|
|     |     | 1   | 2   | 3   | 4   | 5   | 6   |
| 7   | 8   | 9   | 10  | 11  | 12  | 13  |
| 14  | 15  | 16  | 17  | 18  | 19  | 20  |
| 21  | 22  | 23  | 24  | 25  | 26  | 27  |
| 28  | 29  |     |     |     |     |     |

An extra day is added in February in a leap year.

# Time on other planets

Each planet in the Solar System has its own days and years.

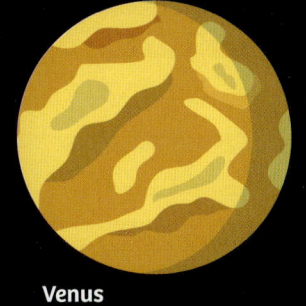

**Venus**

Venus rotates on its axis so slowly that a Venus day (lasting 243 Earth days) is longer than a Venus year (225 Earth days)!

**Jupiter**

At the other extreme, Jupiter rotates so quickly that its day lasts just under 10 Earth hours. One Jupiter year lasts 12 Earth years. There are 10,476 Jupiter days in one Jupiter year!

## Try this!

*What fraction of the year are you at school? Calculate how many weeks' holiday you have, including bank holidays, and remember that you don't go to school at the weekends!* ***Are you at school for more or less than half of the year?***

# Ratios

A ratio tells you how much of one thing there is compared with another.

There are 4 red squares to 1 blue square. This is a ratio of **4 : 1**.

As with equivalent fractions, the number of objects can be scaled up without changing the ratio. These examples all have the ratio **4 : 1**.

## Ratios around you

Computer screens come in different aspect ratios. This is the ratio between the horizontal width and the vertical height.

*A widescreen computer screen has an aspect ratio of 16 : 9.*

Most national flags are rectangles, but their aspect ratios vary. A flag's aspect ratio is given as the ratio between its height and its width.

The US flag has an aspect ratio of 10 : 19.

*The flag of Switzerland has an aspect ratio of 1 : 1. It is a square.*

The flag of China has an aspect ratio of 2 : 3.

## What is the aspect ratio of your national flag?

# Scaling ratios

**To change the scale of a ratio, you multiply both parts of the ratio by the same number.**

### 1 : 8

To scale this ratio by 2, multiply both parts by 2.

### (1 × 2) : (8 × 2)
### 2 : 16

## Following recipes

Cooks use recipes that give the ratios of different ingredients. These need to be scaled up or down, depending on how many people you are cooking for. Here is a recipe for a pancake mix to make six pancakes: **It has a ratio of 1 : 50 : 150.**

1 large egg
50 g flour
150 ml milk

# Try this!

*Parts of your body can be compared using ratios. These ratios are your body's proportions. With the help of a friend, use a tape measure to measure your body. Calculate the ratio between your arm span (arms spread horizontally) and your height. Sitting down, measure your femur (thigh bone) from the hip joint to the edge of your knee. Now calculate the ratio between the length of your femur and your height.*

**Compare your ratios with those of your friends and family. Are they similar?** *In most people, the ratio between arm span and height is about 1 : 1. The ratio between femur length and height is about 1 : 4.*

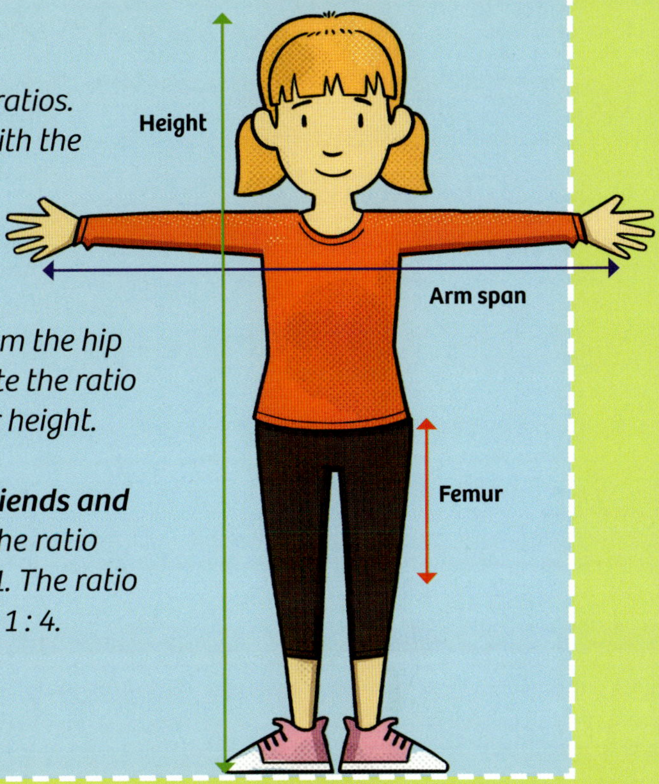

Height

Arm span

Femur

4 large eggs
200 g flour
600 ml milk

If you want to make 24 pancakes, that is four times as many as the recipe. Multiply all the quantities by four. In each case, the ratios between them stay the same.
(1 × 4) : (50 × 4) : (150 × 4) = 4 : 200 : 600

# Scaling up and down

**Scale drawings show an object with its size reduced or enlarged according to a scale, which is written as a ratio.**

height 3 : 1

length 3 : 1

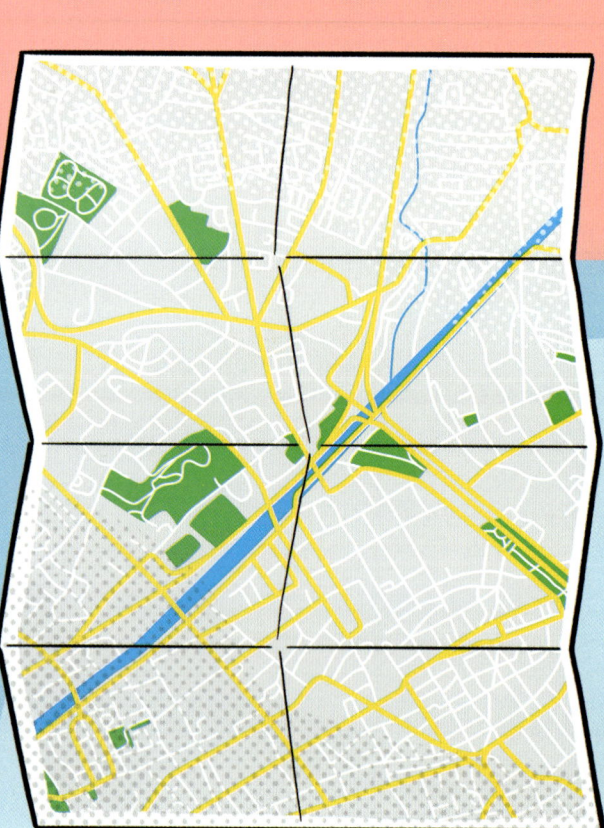

## Making maps

Map-makers create maps with the scale marked on them.

The scale on the map on the left is **1 : 100,000**. This means that 1 cm on the map represents 100,000 cm in the real world, which is 1 km.

The map on the right shows the central town of the same area zoomed in to a scale of **1 : 25,000**. This means that 1 cm on the map represents 25,000 cm in the real world, which is 250 m. As the scale increases, more details can be shown.

This butterfly is drawn to a scale of 3 : 1. The length and width of the drawing are three times longer than the length and width of the original photo.

Shed

## Drawing to scale

To make scale drawings, it helps to use graph paper. In the scale drawing above, each square on the graph paper represents 1 m² (square metre) of real space. It shows a rectangular garden that is 12 m long and 6 m wide. **How long is the path? What is the ratio of the shed's length to its width?**

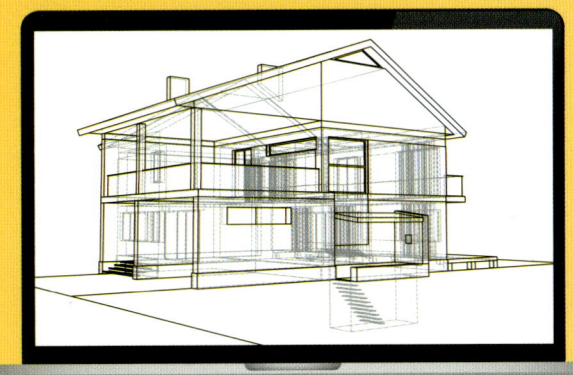

*Architects make scale drawings on computers so that the builders can see what the dimensions of each room should be.*

## Try this!

*Create a scale drawing of your own on graph paper. Measure a room with a tape measure and choose a suitable scale, such as 1 square : 1 m². Draw the room on the graph paper and add in a couple of objects, such as a table or a bed.*

# Percentages

**A percentage is a way of expressing the number of hundredths we have – 'per cent' means 'per 100'. It is written using the % sign.**

1% means 1 part per 100. This can also be expressed as the fraction $\frac{1}{100}$ or the decimal 0.01.

1% of this square is orange.

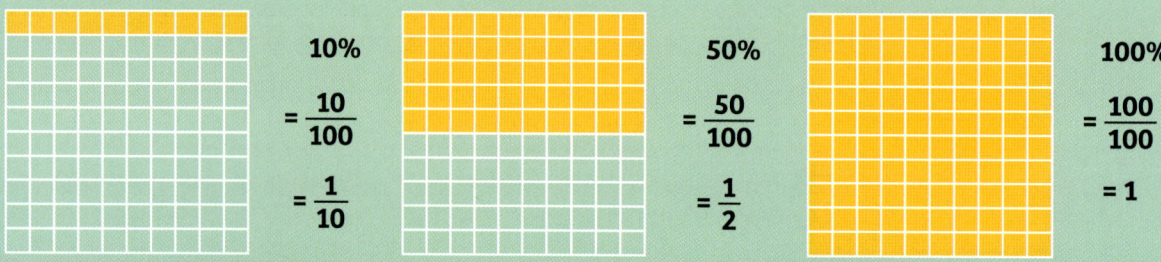

10%

$= \frac{10}{100}$

$= \frac{1}{10}$

50%

$= \frac{50}{100}$

$= \frac{1}{2}$

100%

$= \frac{100}{100}$

$= 1$

A percentage can also be more than 100. If you have 200% of something, that means you have 200 parts per 100, or twice as much.

## Calculating percentages of numbers

To calculate a percentage of a number, first turn your percentage into a fraction with a denominator of 100. Multiply the number by the numerator, then divide the result by 100. For example, in a bag of 150 sweets, 20% are strawberry flavour. **How many strawberry sweets are there?**

20% of 150 $= \frac{20}{100} \times 150 = \frac{3000}{100} = $ **30** strawberry sweets

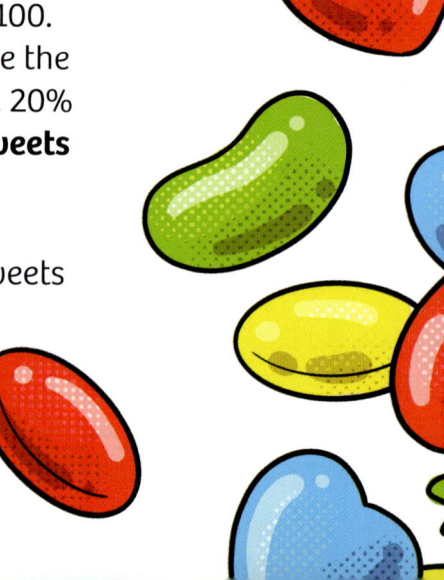

# Percentages around you

Exam results are often worked out as percentages. A pass mark may be 50% or higher, meaning that you got at least half of the questions right.

*Mobile phones display battery life as a percentage of a full charge.*

## Try this!

*Three students – Daisy, Aisha and Mark – sat a maths exam that was marked out of 80. Their marks were as follows:*

Daisy: $\dfrac{38}{80}$ Aisha: $\dfrac{43}{80}$ Mark: $\dfrac{51}{80}$

*If the pass mark was 50%, which of the students passed the exam?*

Answers on page 47

# Percentage discounts

**Shops often announce their sales by advertising the price reduction as a percentage.**

Working out the sale price is easy if everything is 50% off. Just divide all the prices by 2.

Full price : **£60**     Sale price : **£30**

## 50% OFF

## 25% OFF

If the sale price is 25% off the full price, you will pay the remainder, which is 75%.

Full price: **£400**
Sale price: **£300**

£400 × 0.75 = £300

# Buyer beware!

Shops sometimes use a sneaky trick to suggest that their sales are very generous. For instance, they may advertise 'up to 70% off'. Beware of this sign. They are advertising the maximum discount – many items will have much smaller percentage reductions.

**Two for £1**

**UP TO 70% OFF**

Shops often offer discounts if you buy two items. To work out the discount you are receiving, divide the cost of two items by 2 and subtract this number from the price of one item.

For instance, in a sales offer:
• one chocolate bar costs 75p
• two chocolate bars cost £1.

Each of the two chocolate bars costs 50p, which is 25p less than the price of one, or $\frac{1}{3}$ off. That's a 33% discount. But do you really want two bars? If not, the shop is tricking you into spending more money and eating more chocolate!

## Try this!

*A shop is giving a discount of 30% off all its clothes.* **What is the new sales price of these three items?**

T-shirt   £5
Jeans     £10
Trainers £20

Answers on page 47

# Fractions in sport

Fractions appear in many different sports. Fractions are used to divide up games and playing areas. They can also be used to measure how well a player is performing.

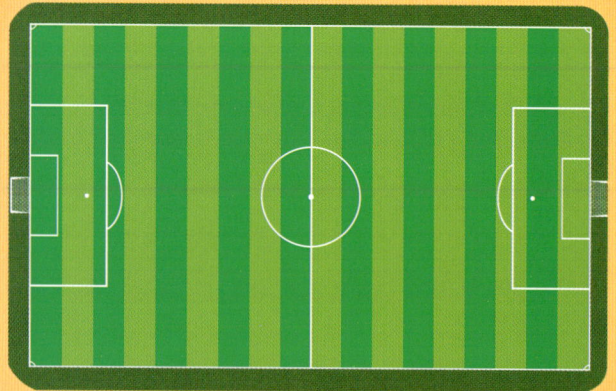

A football (soccer) match is divided into two equal halves of 45 minutes.

### 45 × 2 = **90 minutes**

A football pitch is divided into two equal halves by the halfway line.

An ice hockey match is divided into three equal thirds (called 'periods') of 20 minutes.

### 20 × 3 = **60 minutes**

An ice hockey rink is divided into two equal halves by a dotted red line, and into three zones by two thick blue lines.

An American football match is divided into four quarters of 15 minutes.

### 15 × 4 = **60 minutes**

An American football pitch is 120 yards (110 metres) long. The last 10 yards at either end are the 'end zones'. The rest of the playing area is divided into 100 equal parts by yard lines. Every tenth yard line is a thick white line.

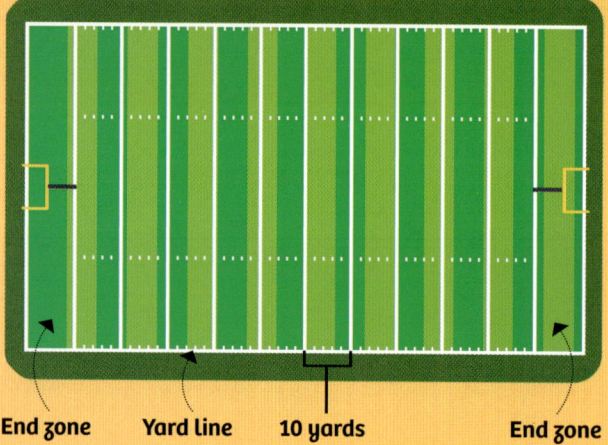

End zone    Yard line    10 yards    End zone

# Knockout competitions

In knock-out competitions, half of the competitors are knocked out in each round. The organisers need to be sure they have the right number of rounds for all the matches. If there are two players in the final, there will be four in the semi-finals, eight in the quarter-finals, etc.

Sixteen competitors compete against each other in a four-round draw. The draw is arranged like this:

**ROUND 1**

Match 1   Match 2   Match 3   Match 4   Match 5   Match 6   Match 7   Match 8

**ROUND 2**

Quarter Final 1   Quarter Final 2   Quarter Final 3   Quarter Final 4

**ROUND 3**

Semi Final 1   Semi Final 2

**ROUND 4**

Final

There are a total of 15 matches, including the final.

## Try this!

*How many rounds are there in a competition with 32 competitors? Draw a table to show each round.* **How many matches are there in total?**

Answers on page 47

# Keeping rhythm

Musicians use fractions to give their music rhythm. The rhythm used is called a time signature and it tells you how many beats there are in each measure (or bar) of music.

## Length of notes

When writing music, the length of a note is indicated by its colour and shape:

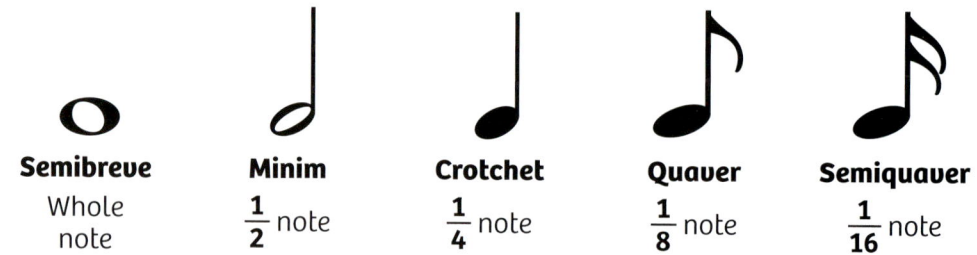

| **Semibreve** | **Minim** | **Crotchet** | **Quaver** | **Semiquaver** |
|---|---|---|---|---|
| Whole note | $\frac{1}{2}$ note | $\frac{1}{4}$ note | $\frac{1}{8}$ note | $\frac{1}{16}$ note |

## Common time

The most common time signature is called $\frac{4}{4}$. Each measure has the length of four quarter note beats. They can contain notes of different lengths or rests (periods of silence). Known as 'common time', this is a great time signature for music. Here are the notes in the first four measures of the tune *Jingle Bells*:

*Jingle Bells*

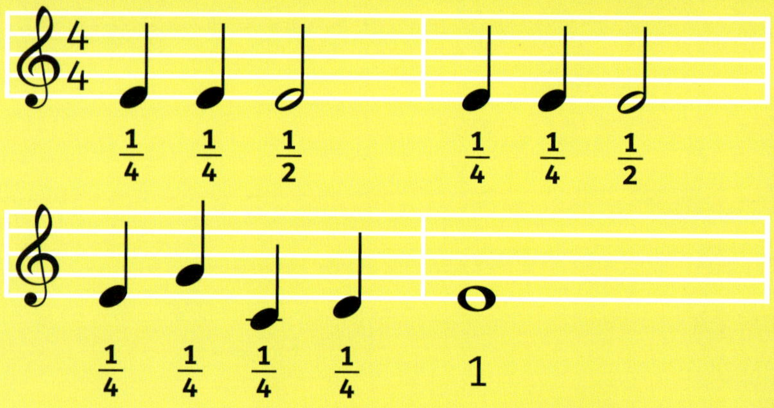

$\frac{1}{4}$    $\frac{1}{4}$    $\frac{1}{2}$      $\frac{1}{4}$    $\frac{1}{4}$    $\frac{1}{2}$

$\frac{1}{4}$    $\frac{1}{4}$    $\frac{1}{4}$    $\frac{1}{4}$      $1$

# Time signatures around you

A march has a time signature of $\frac{2}{4}$. This is the rhythm of our feet as we walk: 'left-right-left-right'. An example of this is the *Wedding March* tune:

*Wedding March*

$\frac{1}{4}$  $\frac{1}{8}$  $\frac{1}{8}$  $\frac{1}{2}$  $\frac{1}{4}$  $\frac{1}{8}$  $\frac{1}{8}$  $\frac{1}{2}$

*My Favourite Things*

$\frac{1}{4}$  $\frac{1}{4}$  $\frac{1}{4}$  $\frac{1}{4}$  $\frac{1}{4}$  $\frac{1}{4}$  $\frac{1}{4}$  $\frac{1}{4}$  $\frac{1}{4}$  $\frac{1}{4}$  $\frac{1}{2}$

A dance called a waltz has a time signature of $\frac{3}{4}$. This gives a rhythm of 'one-two-three, one-two-three'. An example of this is the *My Favourite Things* tune (second line above).

## Try this!

*Clap your hands in time to the beats for each of the tunes. Clapping along gives you a great sense of the rhythm of a piece of music.*

# Egyptian fractions

The ancient Egyptians wrote out every fraction as a sum of fractions with a numerator of 1. These are also known as unit fractions.

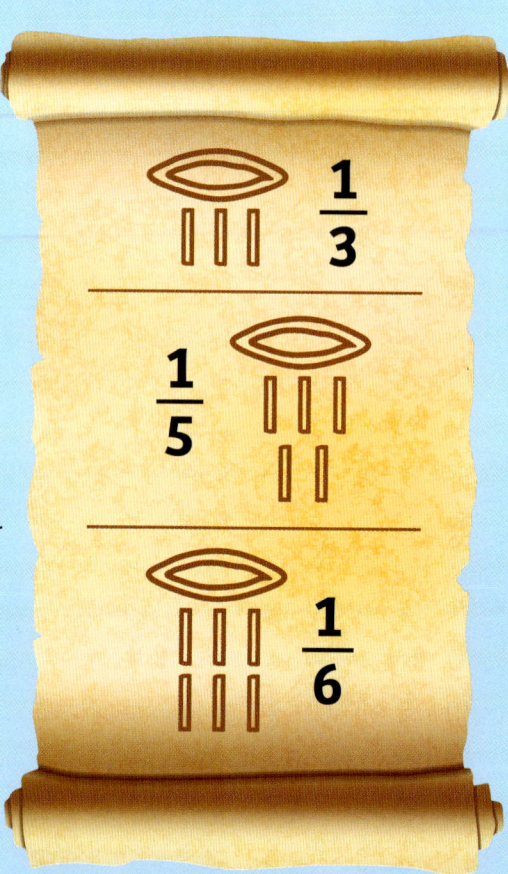

The ancient Egyptians used a writing system called hieroglyphs. They wrote down fractions by placing the symbol for 'mouth' above the denominator.

Each fraction in a sum of Egyptian fractions has a different denominator. For example:

$$\frac{2}{3} = \frac{1}{2} + \frac{1}{6}$$

$$\frac{3}{4} = \frac{1}{2} + \frac{1}{4}$$

$$\frac{6}{7} = \frac{1}{2} + \frac{1}{3} + \frac{1}{42}$$

## Using Egyptian fractions

The ancient Egyptians used unit fractions to divide workers' rations.

For instance, if you have 8 workers and 5 loaves of bread, how do you divide up the loaves among the workers?

Each worker is due $\frac{5}{8}$ of a loaf. You could slice each loaf into eight pieces and give the workers five pieces each, but Egyptian fractions give you a better solution.

$$\frac{5}{8} = \frac{1}{2} + \frac{1}{8}$$

You slice one loaf into eight pieces and the other four in half. Each worker gets two pieces: one $\frac{1}{2}$ and one $\frac{1}{8}$.

# Try this!

*Use Egyptian fractions to solve this sharing problem. You and three friends have ordered three pizzas. You need to share the pizzas out equally between the four of you. How do you do this with the fewest slices?* **How many times do you need to slice each pizza?**

Answers on page 47

# Growing in fractions

**You can create beautiful patterns by adding or subtracting a fraction of a shape in a series of steps.**

A fraction tree grows by repeating a simple process. Its trunk splits into two branches. Each of the branches splits into two more branches. Each of these splits into two again, and so on. This produces a tree with a thick trunk and thin twigs.

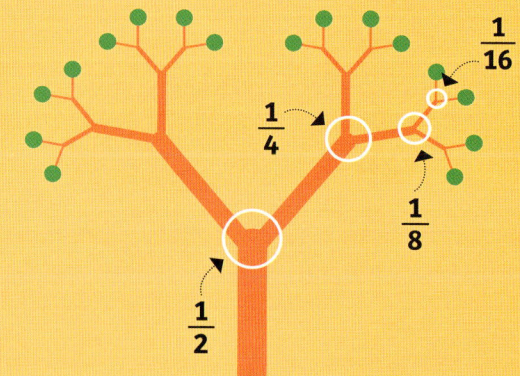

$$\frac{1}{16}$$

$$\frac{1}{4}$$

$$\frac{1}{8}$$

$$\frac{1}{2}$$

*Repeating the process many times creates a beautiful tree shape.*

# Sierpinski triangle

A Sierpinksi triangle forms in a similar way to a fraction tree, but this time you need to subtract a fraction. In this case, you subtract one quarter of the shape each time. Start with an equilateral triangle.

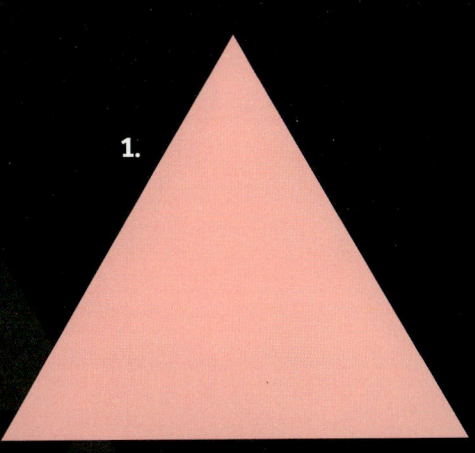

1.

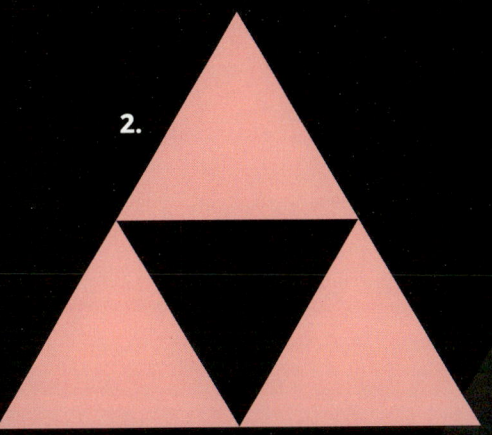

2.

Draw another equilateral triangle with corners at the mid-point on each side of the large triangle. This creates four equilateral triangles. Remove the middle one.

Now repeat the same process with the triangles you have left, and repeat again and again.

3.

4.

5.

6.

# Fractals around us

Shapes such as the fraction tree are shapes that repeat themselves at smaller and smaller scales. These are known in mathematics as fractals. Fractals are all around us in nature.

*The smaller parts of a fern are the same shape as the whole.*

*Each mini-floret on Romanesco broccoli is the same shape as the larger florets.*

When rivers spread out in a delta, they split into smaller streams in a fractal pattern.

*Snowflakes form six-sided fractal shapes.*

# Try this!

*Create your own snowflake on graph paper.*

**1.** *Start by drawing a large equilateral triangle with a pencil. Use a ruler to divide each side of the triangle into thirds and mark the points.*

**2.** *Draw a new equilateral triangle on each side from these points. Carefully rub out the parts of the line shown in black. This will make a six-sided star.*

**3.** *Repeat the same process for the sides of the six smaller triangles.*

**4.** *Repeat the process one more time.*

# Quiz

**1** Which of these shapes is divided into thirds?

a)   b) 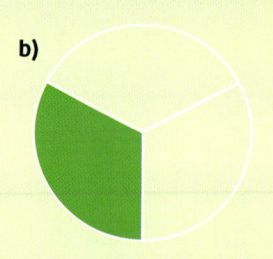  c)

**2** Find the missing number.

a) $3 = \frac{?}{2}$  b) $8 = \frac{24}{?}$  c) $2 = \frac{?}{18}$

**3** Convert the following mixed numbers into improper fractions.

a) $1\frac{1}{3}$  b) $4\frac{3}{4}$  c) $2\frac{1}{2}$

**4** You have $4\frac{1}{2}$ pizzas to divide between 9 people. If each pizza contains 4 slices, how many slices does each person get?

**5** Which of these shapes are split into equal quarters?

a)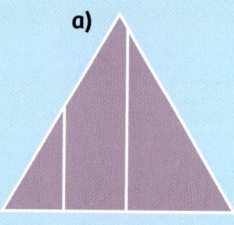

b)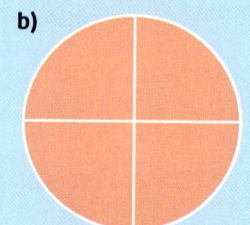

c)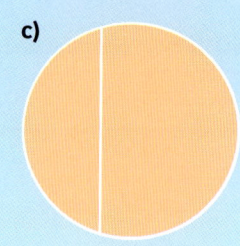

d)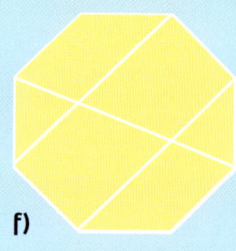

e)

f)

**6** What fractions are represented by the circles on these number lines?

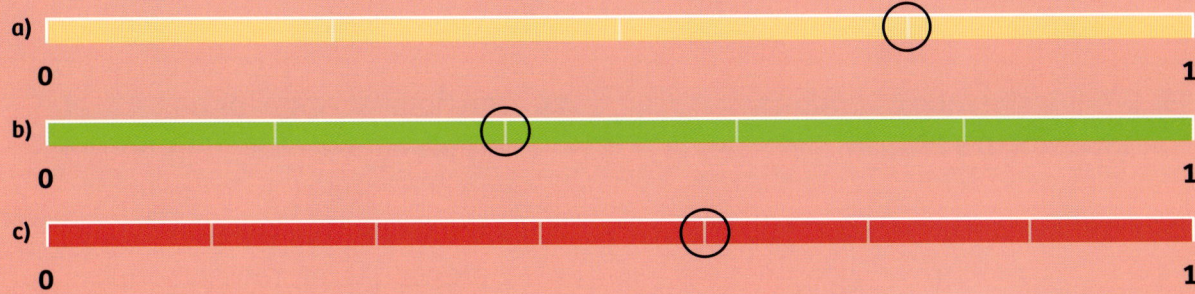

a)
0                                                                 1

b)
0                                                                 1

c)
0                                                                 1

---

**7** a) What fraction of fuel is left in this car's tank?

b) The tank's full capacity is 40 litres.
How many litres of fuel are left?

c) The car can cover 20 kilometres per litre.
**How far can the driver drive before refilling?**

---

**8** Convert the following fractions into decimal fractions:

a) $\frac{3}{10}$  b) $\frac{1}{2}$  c) $\frac{3}{5}$

**9** In your wallet, you have three £1 coins, two £0.10 coins and four £0.01 coins. How much money do you have in total?

---

**10** If a human hair is 50 millionths of a metre wide, how many hairs could be laid side-by-side on a line that is 1 millimetre long? *(Hint: There are 1,000 millionths of a metre in 1 millimetre.)*

**11** Which of the following years was not a leap year?

a) 1900  b) 2000  c) 2020

*(Hint: Turn to page 22 to find the rules for calculating leap years and follow the rules carefully.)*

**12** If it takes you 15 minutes to walk 1 kilometre, how far can you walk in an hour?

**13** What is the ratio of bananas to apples in this basket?

**14** You have a recipe for pasta that requires you to mix flour and egg in a ratio of 3 : 2, meaning 3 grams of flour for every 2 grams of egg. You have two eggs that weigh 50 grams each. How many grams of flour do you need for your mix to make pasta using both eggs?

**15** You have a map showing your town with a scale of 1 : 10,000. If the distance from home to school is 10 centimetres on the map, how far is it in the real world?

**a)** 10 kilometres   **b)** 100 metres   **c)** 1 kilometre

**16** The number of students taking Maths is 50% greater than the number of students taking Geography. If there are 30 Geography students, how many Maths students are there?

**17** In a closing-down sale, every item in a shop is marked at 80% off. Yihan has £10 to spend in the shop. At full price, jeans cost £40, while packs of socks cost £5. If Yihan buys a pair of jeans, how many packs of socks can she buy?

**18** A knock-out tennis tournament has 64 competitors. How many matches does the winner of the tournament play?

**19** Alfie has 12 marbles. Lucas has no marbles. If Alfie gives one third of his marbles to Lucas, how many marbles does Alfie have left? What is the ratio between Alfie's marbles and Lucas's marbles?

**20** Fill in the blanks in the following sums:

a) $\frac{1}{3} + \frac{1}{4} = ?$

b) $\frac{1}{2} + ? = \frac{3}{4}$

c) $\frac{1}{4} + ? = \frac{1}{2}$

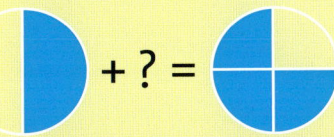

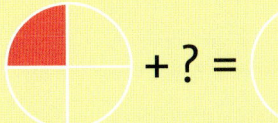

# Answers

# Index